THE ENRON COLLAPSE

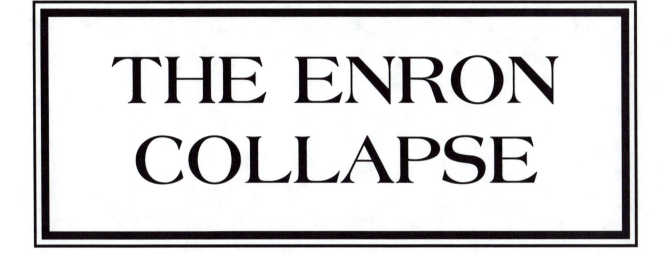

THE ENRON COLLAPSE

Gregory J. Jenkins

Pearson
Education

Upper Saddle River, New Jersey 07458

Acquisitions editor: Thomas Sigel
Assistant editor: Jessica Romeo
Production editor: Carol Zaino
Manufacturer: Technical Communication Services

ISBN 0-13-046332-9

10 9 8 7 6 5 4 3 2 1

TABLE OF CONTENTS

PREFACE

The devil's in the details.
-Unknown

Never before has there been a bankruptcy of a U.S. corporation as large as Enron. With a global reach and worldwide assets of more than $65 billion in 2000, Enron did not seem in danger of collapsing under a wave of accounting scandals. The full scope of the details surrounding Enron's demise is still not completely known. Investigations are being conducted by the U.S. Departments of Justice and Labor and the Securities and Exchange Commission. No less than a half-dozen Congressional committees either have or are in the process of conducting hearings into the company's collapse. Then there are the countless private inquiries being conducted by attorneys and investigators retained by investors, creditors, and others in the hopes of recovering the billions of dollars in losses.

It is my hope that this monograph will give context and meaning to the Enron failure. As this is written, there are literally thousands of former Enron employees who have lost their jobs and much, if not all, of their retirement savings. In addition, Arthur Andersen, a well-respected accounting firm that has served clients for more than 89 years is reeling from its involvement in the Enron audits. As you read the following pages think of the men and women who are Enron and Andersen.

ACKNOWLEDGMENTS

I want to thank to Barb Chaney and Bruce Branson both of whom served as sounding boards on numerous occasions over the last several months. I also want to express my heartfelt thanks to my wife Elaine whose understanding and patience allowed me to accept and complete this project in spite of our overly busy schedule.

INTRODUCTION

The Enron bankruptcy has thrust the accounting profession into the public spotlight in a most unflattering way. The profession now finds itself in a position of having to defend standards and rules that have heretofore seldom been the subject of such intense public scrutiny. There is little doubt that some of the impending changes (e.g., changes in consolidation requirements for special-purpose entities) are probably overdue, but other potential changes (e.g., prohibition of certain non audit services) are more likely to be a reaction to the current political climate.

The following are short summaries of several important issues that have arisen from the Enron collapse. The summaries are intended primarily to make you aware of the "big picture" issues. While each of these issues is discussed in more detail in the following pages, you should consult authoritative guidance such as the Financial Accounting Standards Board's (FASB) *Current Text* and the American Institute of Certified Public Accountant's (AICPA) *Professional Standards* for additional information on specific accounting and auditing issues.

- Special-purpose entities – Special-purpose entities (SPEs) have received relatively little attention by most accountants in the past; however, they are now squarely at the center of the largest corporate bankruptcy in U.S. history. SPEs are typically established so that a company can form a joint venture with other interested parties to carry out a specific transaction or series of transactions without subjecting the other parties to the risks more generally associated with the company's operations. U.S. generally accepted accounting principles (GAAP) allow companies to record the gains and losses of SPEs without reporting their assets and liabilities in certain instances. By not consolidating certain SPEs Enron avoided adding more than $1 billion of debt to its balance sheet. Circumstances now indicate that the company failed to follow GAAP for some significant SPEs.

- Related party transactions – In the normal course of business, transactions are presumed to be conducted at arm's length. In other words, companies conduct and negotiate transactions in such a way as to provide themselves with the most advantageous terms possible. While most transactions are conducted in this manner, transactions that occur between related parties cannot be presumed to have occurred at arm's length. Consequently, the disclosure and accounting for these transactions must be scrutinized very carefully not only by management, but also by the company's auditor. Hindsight suggests that Enron's disclosure of related party transactions was woefully inadequate.

- Corporate governance – Sound corporate governance principles require the active and meaningful participation of both management and the board of directors (BOD) in a company's affairs. Effective corporate governance manifests itself in the design and implementation of a system of internal controls. Whereas management is responsible for the day-to-day operations and functioning of internal controls, the BOD serves a unique and important oversight role by providing an "independent check" on a company's management. A company's BOD commonly fulfills its oversight role through various committees including audit committees, finance committees, and compensation committees. Following the company's bankruptcy, Enron's BOD appointed a Special Investigation Committee (SIC) to conduct a comprehensive review of certain transactions between Enron and various partnerships established and managed by the company's former chief financial officer. The SIC concluded that there had been a breakdown in the company's corporate governance system and that oversight of the transactions by "Enron's Board of Directors and Management failed for many reasons."

1

- Audit documentation – Andersen has been indicted by the U.S. Department of Justice for obstruction of justice in connection with the destruction of documents related to the Enron audit. The firm has publicly stated that its record retention policy was clear as to the steps that firm personnel should have taken to preserve all documentation related to the Enron audit once the firm became aware of the pending SEC investigation. At press time there had been no public announcement regarding either the exact quantity or types of documents that were destroyed; however, Andersen has said that it has no evidence that any actual audit documentation (i.e., working papers) was destroyed. Although valid, this distinction seems to have resulted in a good measure of confusion regarding the nature of audit documentation.

- Self-regulatory status – The accounting profession has been largely self-regulating for many years; however, Enron's collapse seems all but certain to end this. The SEC began discussing a new regulatory structure with representatives of the Big Five accounting firms and the AICPA within days of Enron's bankruptcy. In addition, several bills have been proposed in both the U.S. House and Senate that propose various changes to the profession's regulatory structure.

THE KEY PLAYERS

The details of Enron's accounting games are still unclear. However, what is clear is that there were certain individuals in key decision-making positions within the company who either must have known or should have known about the company's affairs. As the investigation of the Enron collapse continues, a number of the following individuals have refused to cooperate with investigative bodies and have invoked their Fifth Amendment right against self-incrimination, while others have testified before various Congressional committees providing their perspective on the company's demise.

- Kenneth (Ken) Lay – Of the individuals at the center of the Enron scandal, Ken Lay is the person who had the most time and energy invested in Enron. Lay's involvement with the company dates back to the company's founding in 1985. He served as Enron's chief executive officer (CEO) from February 1986 until February 2001 and then again from August 2001 until he resigned in January 2002. In addition, Lay was the Chairman of the BOD from February 1986 until February 2002.

- Jeffrey (Jeff) Skilling – Jeff Skilling was a partner at the prestigious consulting firm of McKinsey & Company when he accepted a position with Enron. As a successful business consultant and graduate of the Harvard Business School, Skilling was viewed by many as an imminently capable and hard-charging executive. He served Enron in a variety of positions prior to his being appointed president and chief operating officer in January 1997. Slightly more than four years later, in February 2001, Skilling was appointed Enron's CEO. He resigned shortly thereafter on August 14, 2001, for "personal reasons."

- Andrew (Andy) Fastow – Andy Fastow began his career with Enron in 1990. Like Skilling, he was seen as an intelligent and innovative manager. Fastow served Enron in a variety of positions prior to his being named senior vice president of finance in January 1997 and chief financial officer (CFO) in March 1998. Fastow was instrumental in forming and, in some instances, managing the partnerships that are at the heart of the Enron scandal. He earned an MBA from the Kellogg Graduate School of Management at Northwestern

University and was employed by Continental Illinois Bank's Asset Securitization Group prior to joining Enron. Fastow was removed as Enron's CFO in October 2001.

- Richard (Rick) Buy – As Enron's chief risk officer, Buy was in a unique position to evaluate many of the transactions that ultimately led to Enron's collapse. He was charged by the Enron BOD with reviewing transactions with certain Fastow partnerships (e.g., LJM partnerships) - a responsibility that was, according to the report of the Special Investigation Committee (commonly known as the Powers Report), either not understood completely or not taken very seriously. Buy was named Enron's chief risk officer in March 1999.

- Richard (Rick) Causey – Rick Causey was named Enron's chief accounting and information officer in January 1997. Causey had also been charged by the Enron BOD with reviewing all LJM transactions. Like Buy, Causey appears to have taken less care with this responsibility than was warranted given the BOD's reliance on his review of the transactions. Causey told the Special Investigation Committee that he understood his responsibility to be primarily to ensure that deal approval sheets related to the LJM transactions contained all necessary signatures.

- Michael Kopper – Kopper had built some impressive credentials before joining Enron in 1994. After earning degrees from two prestigious universities, Duke University and the London School of Economics, he gained experience in structuring complex project financings for a variety of companies at both Chemical Bank and Toronto Dominion Bank. He leveraged this experience in his positions with the Enron Global Finance (EGF) group. Given his experience with complex financing arrangements, it is not surprising that Fastow asked Kopper to manage Chewco Investments, L.P., the first of several questionable partnerships arranged by Fastow. Kopper resigned from Enron in July 2001.

- Sherron Watkins – Sherron Watkins was named as a *Time's* "Person of the Week" in January 2002 for her part in exposing the accounting games at Enron. On the other hand, Watkins has reportedly endured criticism from both current and past Enron employees for what they view as her "role" in the company's collapse. Regardless of how she is viewed, the now famous letter that began simply "Dear Mr. Lay" was not only insightful and to the point, but also prescient in its statement that Enron would "implode in a wave of accounting scandals."

- David Duncan – Much to the dismay of many observers, David Duncan invoked his Fifth Amendment right when he appeared before the U.S. House of Representative's Committee on Energy and Commerce. As Andersen's lead partner on the Enron audit, he was privy to a vast amount of information regarding Enron's financial statements. In April 2002, Duncan reached an agreement with the U.S. Department of Justice under which he agreed to plead guilty of obstructing justice.

- Arthur Andersen LLP – Andersen was indicted in March 2002 by the U.S. Department of Justice on one count of obstruction of justice in connection with its destruction of Enron-related documents. Shortly thereafter, the firm's CEO and managing partner Joe Berardino announced his resignation. Andersen, long considered one of the most stable and successful accounting firms in the world, is now reeling from client losses and the Enron scandal. The firm's future is uncertain.

THE TRANSFORMATION PROCESS

Enron Corporation was created by the 1985 merger of Houston Natural Gas and InterNorth, a natural gas company based in Omaha, Nebraska. Prior to their merger, each of these companies was engaged in essentially the same business – transporting and selling natural gas. The merger of these two companies created a massive network of some 37,000 miles of pipe and gave birth to the first nationwide gas pipeline system. Although such a vast network might have ordinarily given the company a significant competitive advantage, the deregulation of the natural gas markets acted to offset this potential boon by eliminating Enron's ability to claim exclusive use of its pipeline system.

In February 1986 after the merger was completed, Ken Lay was named as the new company's CEO and chairman of the board. The new CEO began to envision a company that was more than just a dominant player in the natural gas market. Before the two companies merged, Houston Natural Gas and InterNorth, like other energy companies, had focused primarily on the generation of revenues and profits through the efficient and effective use of traditional assets (e.g., power generating plants, gas pipelines, etc.). Deregulation of the nation's energy markets created tremendous challenges for the new company. It set the stage for the transformation of Enron from a traditional energy company into an unregulated utilities-focused investment company.

Lay realized the company had to evolve if it were to succeed in the new environment, so the company retained the consulting firm of McKinsey & Co. Jeff Skilling was the McKinsey & Co. consultant who arrived to help the young company. Skilling recommended that Enron leverage its size and resources by essentially creating its own natural gas market. Enron could do this by buying gas from various suppliers and selling gas to interested buyers and doing so through contractual arrangements that would ensure costs and prices. The use of contracts allowed Enron to control more fully its revenues and expenses. This was not only a brilliant marketing strategy, but also a strategy which provided the company and investment community strong and predictable earnings.

Lay was so impressed with Skilling that he made him the proverbial "offer he couldn't refuse." In August 1990, Skilling accepted the position of chairman and CEO of the newly formed Enron Finance Corporation. Over the next six years, he served Enron in several capacities, always delivering superior performance. In January 1997, Skilling received a significant promotion when he was appointed as Enron's president and chief operating officer. Some have suggested that there was an effective passing of the torch from Lay to Skilling at this time. Regardless of whether this is true, it seems clear that Skilling was being groomed as the company's next CEO. Finally, Skilling's hard work paid off in February 2001 with the announcement that he would take over as CEO from Ken Lay, who was stepping down from the position after more than fifteen years.

Enron underwent dramatic changes in the 1990s. The transformation seems to have been partly a result of a convergence of factors – an extended bull market, a relatively young management team, and tremendous interest and growth in the high tech industry. During the late 1990s, Enron appeared to have the Midas touch. While revenues grew from slightly more than $9 billion in 1995 to an astounding $101 billion in 2000, Enron was also becoming a different company. Management recognized this reality when, in its Letter to Shareholders in the 1999 Annual Report, it said, "Enron is moving so fast that sometimes others have trouble defining us. But we know who we are. We are clearly a knowledge-based company, and the skills and resources we used to transform the energy business are proving to be equally valuable in other businesses." As shown in Figure 1, the changes and the apparently strong earnings performance were rewarded by Wall Street with an ever-increasing stock price. From early 1997 to late 2000, Enron's common stock price grew from approximately $20 per share to almost $90 per share. Throughout this time period the company evolved from a traditional energy company into a company that not only produced and distributed energy, but also traded commodities such as wood fiber, steel, electricity, natural gas, weather futures, and Internet bandwidth. It now appears as though the growing emphasis on trading activities was a catalyst for some of the key decisions that ultimately led to Enron's collapse.

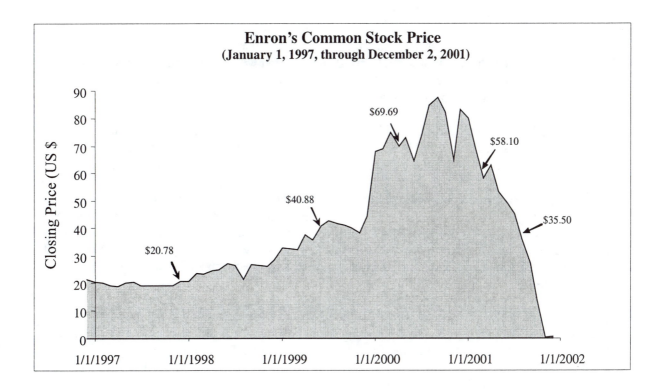

Note: Month-end closing stock prices were obtained from publicly available data sources. Closing prices reflect the effects of all stock splits/dividends.

Figure 1

SHERRON WATKINS

On August 15, 2001, Sherron Watkins made a decision that changed her life when she sent a one-page anonymous letter to Ken Lay who had just resumed the office of CEO after the unexpected resignation of Jeff Skilling (see Figure 2 for an excerpt of the letter). At the time she wrote the letter, Watkins was working for Andy Fastow to identify assets that Enron may want to consider selling. She had just returned to work at Enron after leaving the company earlier in the year as part of a downsizing in the broadband division.

Dear Mr. Lay,

Has Enron become a risky place to work? For those of us who didn't get rich over the last few years, can we afford to stay?

Skilling's abrupt departure will raise suspicions of accounting improprieties and valuation issues. Enron has been very aggressive in its accounting – most notably the Raptor transactions and the Condor vehicle. We do have valuation issues with our international assets and possibly some of our EES MTM positions.

The spotlight will be on us, the market just can't accept that Skilling is leaving his dream job. I think that the valuation issues can be fixed and reported with other goodwill write-downs to occur in 2002. How do we fix the Raptor and Condor deals? They unwind in 2002 and 2003, we will have to pony up Enron stock and that won't go unnoticed.

To the layman on the street, it will look like we recognized funds flow of $800 mm from merchant asset sales in 1999 by selling to a vehicle (Condor) that we capitalized with a promise of Enron stock in later years. Is that really funds flow or is it cash from equity issuance?

We have recognized over $550 million of fair value gains on stocks via our swaps with Raptor, much of that stock has declined significantly – Avici by 98%, from $178 mm to $5 mm, The New Power Co by 70%, from $20/share to $6/share. The value in the swaps won't be there for Raptor, so once again Enron will issue stock to offset these losses. Raptor is an LJM entity. It sure looks to the layman on the street that we are hiding losses in a related company and will compensate that company with Enron stock in the future.

I am incredibly nervous that we will implode in a wave of accounting scandals. My 8 years of Enron work history will be worth nothing on my resume, the business world will consider the past successes as nothing but an elaborate accounting hoax. Skilling is resigning for 'personal reasons' but I think he wasn't having fun, looked down the road and knew this stuff was unfixable and would rather abandon ship now than resign in shame in 2 years.

Is there a way our accounting guru's [sic] can unwind these deals now? I have thought and thought about how to do this, but I keep bumping into one big problem – we booked the Condor and Raptor deals in 1999 and 2000, we enjoyed a wonderfully high stock price, many executives sold stock, we then try and reverse or fix the deals in 2001 and it's a bit like robbing the bank in one year and trying to pay back it [sic] back 2 years later. Nice try, but investors were hurt, they bought at $70 and $80/share looking for $120/share and now they're at $38 or worse. We are under too much scrutiny and there are probably one or two disgruntled 'redeployed' employees who know enough about the 'funny' accounting to get us in trouble.

Figure 2

Watkins's letter led to a conversation between Lay and James Derrick, Enron's General Counsel, regarding the need to retain an outside party to conduct an investigation. Lay and Derrick decided that they would ask Vinson & Elkins (V&E) to conduct an investigation. The two also determined that the investigation should be of a somewhat limited scope with the primary purpose of assessing whether a full investigation should be performed. The decision to limit the investigation was significant because V&E was told that their work should not specifically consider the accounting treatment of specific transactions or the accounting advice provided by Andersen.

On October 15, 2001, just one day before the company was set to announce the results of its third quarter, V&E delivered its report to Enron. According to the Powers Report, the V&E analysis listed four main areas about which Watkins had expressed concerns in her letter: the conflict of interests related to Andy Fastow's dual role as Enron CFO and LJM manager; the accounting treatment of the Raptor transactions; the sufficiency of the Raptor transactions' disclosures; and the financial statement impact of the transactions. The law firm concluded that it had found no evidence that the apparent conflict of interest had resulted in economic harm to Enron. With respect to the accounting matters, the analysis stated that both Enron and Andersen recognized "that the accounting treatment on the Condor/Whitewing and Raptor transactions is creative and aggressive, but no one has reason to believe that it is inappropriate from a technical standpoint." The firm went on to conclude that its investigation did not warrant a "further widespread investigation by independent counsel or auditors."

THE UNRAVELING OF ENRON

Appearing before the U.S. House of Representatives' Committee on Energy and Commerce Jeff Skilling said that when he resigned as CEO on August 14, 2001, he had no reason to doubt that the company was in excellent financial condition. When asked by members of the U.S. House of Representatives' Committee on Energy and Commerce why Enron failed, Skilling appeared pensive and then said that he believed the company's collapse was simply due to an old-fashioned run on the bank that resulted from market participants losing confidence in Enron. Although accurate, the simplicity of this response discounts the effects of the unraveling of the complex ruse that actually led to the "run on the bank."

Enron announced its earnings for the third quarter of 2001 on Tuesday, October 16, 2001. The company's earnings announcement contained a significant and unwelcome surprise – "non-recurring charges of $1.01 billion." These non recurring charges consisted of three separate items, the last of which was described in the press release as "$544 million related to losses associated with certain investments, principally Enron's interest in The New Power Company, broadband and technology investments, and early termination during the third quarter of certain structured finance arrangements with a previously disclosed entity." This charge related to transactions between Enron and LJM2, a partnership that had been created and managed by Andy Fastow while he was Enron's chief financial officer. The investment community reacted swiftly and predictably. Enron's stock closed that afternoon at $33.84 per share, but by the end of the week the share price had declined by 23% to close at $26.05. Less than a week later, on October 22, Enron announced that the SEC had requested information related to the company's transactions with LJM2. Later that day the company's stock closed at $20.65. Just two days later, Enron announced that Andy Fastow was being replaced as the company's CFO. By the end of the week, on October 26, Enron's stock closed at $15.40 – a loss in value of more than 54% in less than two weeks! However, there was more bad news to come.

The proverbial "straw that broke the camel's back" came in the form of an 8-K filing on November 8. In its SEC filing, the company announced that it planned to restate its financial statements for 1997 through 2000 and the first two quarters of 2001 because of the required consolidation of certain previously unconsolidated entities. The company stated that the expected effects would "include a reduction to reported net income of approximately $96 million in 1997, $113 million in 1998, $250 million in 1999, and $132 million in 2000, increases of $17 million for the first quarter of 2001 and $5 million for the second quarter and a reduction of $17 million for the third quarter of 2001." To put these amounts in perspective, consider that these amounts represented reductions in reported earnings of *91%* in 1997, *16%* in 1998, *28%* in 1999, and *13%* in 2000. The restatement also included an "increase in Enron's debt by approximately $711 million in 1997, $561 million in 1998, $685 million in 1999 and $628 million in 2000." Enron never recovered from the series of bad news events and eventually filed for bankruptcy protection under Chapter 11 on December 2, 2001.

THE SPE TRANSACTIONS

On October 28, 2001, following the announcement of its third quarter earnings, Enron's BOD established the Special Investigation Committee (SIC) to investigate the facts and circumstances surrounding the related party transactions conducted between Enron and various partnerships created and managed by Andy Fastow. The Powers Report, as the SIC's report has become known, consists of numerous pages of transaction analysis and commentary. What follows is a summary of several of the most significant transactions as explained in the Powers Report. Figure 3 provides further context for the following transactions by showing Enron's stock price over the affected periods.

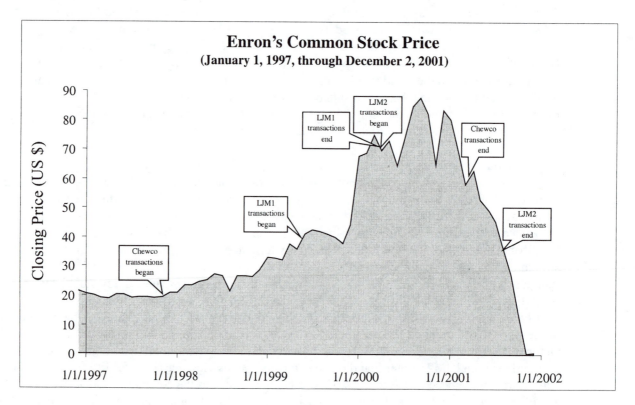

Note: Month-end closing stock prices were obtained from publicly available data sources. Closing prices reflect the effects of all stock splits/dividends.

Figure 3

Chewco Investments, L.P.

From 1993 to 1997, Enron and California Public Employees' Retirement System (CalPERS) were invested in a joint venture called Joint Energy Development Investment, L.P., or JEDI. Because JEDI had been formed as a joint venture and the partners exercised joint control, Enron did not consolidate JEDI into its financial statements. Consequently, generally accepted accounting principles required Enron to record gains and losses from JEDI's operations, but not to record its assets and liabilities. The only asset that Enron was required to show for JEDI was the amount of its investment – $250 million in stock.

After several years, Enron began to entertain the idea of forming another partnership – JEDI II – in which CalPERS would be invited to invest. Notwithstanding what it viewed as an excellent investment opportunity, Enron was concerned that CalPERS would be hesitant to invest in another partnership while simultaneously holding such a large investment in JEDI. Because Enron was committed to JEDI II, the company decided to assist CalPERS in selling its investment in JEDI; however, Enron did not want to jeopardize JEDI's status as an unconsolidated entity. Accordingly, Fastow, who had been named Enron's executive vice president of finance earlier in the year, proposed that he create and manage a limited partnership to purchase CalPERS's investment in JEDI. The new arrangement was dubbed "Chewco."

After concerns were raised regarding the need to disclose Fastow's involvement with Chewco in the company's proxy statement, Fastow recruited Michael Kopper, another Enron employee who reported to him, to manage the partnership. The company did not have to disclose Kopper's involvement with Chewco in its proxy statement; however, according to Enron's Code of Conduct of Business Affairs, his role did require approval by the CEO and chairman. According to the Powers Report, there is no evidence that this approval was ever obtained, or that the BOD was ever made aware of Kopper's involvement with the partnership.

In November 1997, after a relatively short negotiation, Enron (via Chewco) agreed to redeem CalPERS' investment in JEDI for $383 million. The terms provided CalPERS with a profit of $133 million on its initial investment of $250 million. The transaction was completed by executing a bridge, or temporary, financing arrangement under which Chewco borrowed all of the necessary proceeds, $383 million, to purchase CalPERS' investment in JEDI. The loans were guaranteed by Enron. At the time of the JEDI partnership redemption, it was understood that Chewco would have to be consolidated into Enron's financial statements unless another financing structure could be arranged before the end of the year – which was less than two months away.

Enron's Attempts to Avoid Consolidation. Enron had to address two issues if it were to avoid consolidating Chewco in its 1997 financial statements – control and outside equity. Each of these issues appears to have received considerable time and attention from Enron employees and outside advisors in the waning days of the year. With respect to control, Enron and Kopper made two changes to Chewco's structure. First, Chewco was converted from a limited liability company (LLC) to a limited liability partnership (LLP) in which Kopper would serve as the general partner. This change was made so that the partnership document could be written in such a way as to place limitations on the general partner's ability to control major partnership policies. Second, Kopper eliminated his formal ownership interest in Chewco's limited partner by transferring his interest in Big River Funding LLC to a friend.

It appears as though the outside equity requirement was more problematic for Enron. According to the Powers Report, efforts to secure outside equity investments were unsuccessful. With 1997 coming to an end, Enron made changes to Chewco's capital structure that it believed met the equity requirements and allowed it to avoid consolidating Chewco (and JEDI) in its financial statements. The new Chewco capital structure included the following:

- A $240 million unsecured subordinated loan to Chewco from Barclays Bank, which Enron guaranteed.
- A $132 million advance from JEDI to Chewco under a revolving credit agreement.
- $11.5 million in equity from Chewco's general partner and limited partners.

The $11.5 million represented approximately 3% of Chewco's equity; however, no third parties ever invested in the entity. Instead, the $11.5 was comprised of an investment of approximately $115,000 from Kopper and $11.4 in "equity loans" to Big River Funding LLC and Little River Funding LLC, Chewco's limited partners, from Barclays Bank. At some point prior to the closing of the loans, Barclays became concerned about the ability of Big River and Little River to repay their "loans," and so it required them to establish cash reserve accounts in the amount of $6.6 million. The cash reserve requirement eliminated the *at risk* nature of more than half of the $11.4 originally invested by Big River and Little River. This fact should have been recognized by Enron and its outside advisors and should have caused the company to consolidate Chewco *and* JEDI into its financial statements beginning in 1997.

The Financial Statement Impact. Enron reaped significant financial rewards from its relationships with Chewco and JEDI. The rewards came in three forms: a guaranty fee, management fees, and investment income. The guaranty fee, $10 million plus a fee based on the loan balance, resulted from Enron's agreement to guarantee Barclays Bank's $240 million loan to Chewco. From late 1997 through 1998, Enron accelerated the recognition of revenue from this arrangement and recorded income of $17.4 million. GAAP required Enron to recognize the guaranty fee over the guaranty period, which it did not. The second source of income was the annual management fee that JEDI agreed to pay to Enron beginning December 1997. This amount was calculated as the greater of $2 million or 2.5% of $383 million (the amount Chewco paid to redeem CalPERS interest in JEDI) less any distributions received by Chewco. Several months later, in March 1998, the agreement was amended to convert 80% of the annual fee to a required payment. This led Enron to record a $28 million asset and recognize income of $25.7 million. Again, Enron inappropriately accelerated the recognition of revenue and failed to recognize the income from this transaction as GAAP required – which in this case would have been as "services" were provided to Chewco.

The most surprising source of income came from Enron's recording the appreciation in its own stock. Recall that Enron and CalPERS had originally formed JEDI by contributing $250 million in Enron stock and $250 million in cash, respectively. Further, recall that the joint venture was controlled equally by both parties and Enron accounted for JEDI using the equity method. Although the use of the equity method was appropriate, it is unclear what basis (i.e., GAAP standard) the company used to record income resulting from the appreciation in its own stock.

According to the Powers Report, the SIC was not able to determine how much income Enron recognized from appreciation in Enron stock held by JEDI from 1993 through 2000; however, its review of audit documentation prepared by Andersen for the first quarter of 2000 indicated that the company recognized income of $126 million for that quarter. If this is correct, then the net income of $338 million reported on Enron's Form 10-Q for the first quarter of 2000 was overstated by $126 million, or 37%. Interestingly, audit documentation from the third quarter of 2000 stated "that income from Enron stock held by JEDI could no longer be recorded on Enron's income statement." This decision preceded the precipitous drop in Enron's stock price that began in early 2001. Had this decision not been made, Enron would have recorded a loss of $90 million in the first quarter of 2001 (Powers Report, 59).

LJM Cayman, L.P. and LJM2 Co-Investment L.P.

Hindsight suggests that the creation of the LJM partnerships was part of a concerted effort by certain Enron employees to manage the company's earnings. These partnerships were described to the BOD as relatively benign vehicles that Enron could use to hedge some of its investments and possibly purchase assets that it wanted to sell. Although the BOD understood these potential benefits, Andy Fastow's active role in the creation and management of each partnership was the source of some concern. Fastow, however, assured the BOD that his partnership responsibilities would not adversely affect Enron's interests. After brief discussions, the BOD, on two separate occasions, ratified Ken Lay's determination that Fastow's participation in LJM1 and LJM2 did not present unacceptable conflicts of interest.

LJM Cayman, L.P. (LJM1). In March 1998, Enron paid $10 million for 5.4 million shares of stock in a privately held Internet service provider called Rhythms NetConnections, Inc. Within fifteen months, Rhythms had gone public and its stock was trading in the mid $50s. In May 1999, Enron's investment was worth almost $300 million; however, the company could not sell its shares until the end of the year because of a lock-up agreement. In addition, Enron was exposed to potential fluctuations in Rhythms stock price because, as a trading security, the investment had to be marked to market. Eager to protect the enormous gains in the Rhythms investment, Jeff Skilling requested that Fastow devise a means to hedge against future losses in its value.

Fastow and Ben Glisan, another Enron employee, formulated a strategy to leverage the increased value of Enron's own stock to hedge the company's Rhythms position. Their plan called for the creation of a limited partnership SPE that would be capitalized with appreciated Enron stock from forward contracts that Enron had with an investment bank. The plan further called for Fastow to create and manage the partnership. On June 28, 1999, Enron's BOD approved the transaction and approved Fastow's involvement as the general partner of LJM1. The final transaction was structured as follows: Enron transferred 3.4 million shares of its own stock to LJM1 in exchange for a $64 million note receivable. In addition, LJM1 received $16 million from "outside parties" so that Enron could satisfy the SPE rules that required a minimum of 3% outside equity to avoid consolidation. LJM1 then capitalized LJM Swap Sub, L.P. by transferring 1.6 million shares of Enron stock it had received from Enron and $3.75 million. Finally, LJM Swap Sub gave Enron a put option on its Rhythms investment under which it agreed to purchase the stock for $56 per share in June 2004. Figure 4 presents a diagram of this transaction.

This transaction did not afford Enron the protection it desired from fluctuations in Rhythms's stock price. After repeated attempts to improve the hedge's effectiveness failed, Skilling made the decision to unwind the transaction. In April 2000, Enron and LJM Swap Sub reached a final agreement on the termination of the transaction. The terms were quite generous to LJM Swap Sub. In exchange for terminating the Rhythms option, LJM Swap Sub returned the Enron stock that it had originally received from LJM1 to Enron, but retained the $3.75 million it had received from LJM1 *and* Enron paid $16.7 million to LJM Swap Sub. To say it more plainly, LJM Swap Sub received $20.45 million from Enron to execute a hedge that was ineffective. Even more surprisingly, LJM1 was allowed to keep the shares of Enron stock that it had originally received from Enron when the transaction was consummated in June 1999. Because of Enron's generosity, LJM1 walked away with stock that was worth $251 million for which it had paid $64 million.

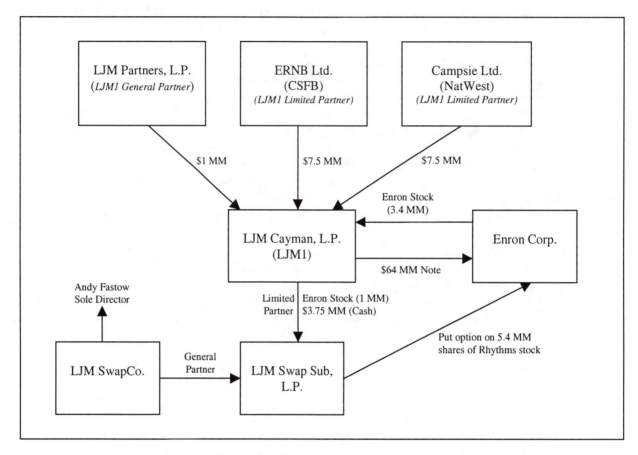

Source: Powers Report, 81.

Figure 4

Problems with LJM1 and Swap Sub. Enron's hedge transaction with LJM Swap Sub was not only ineffective because it failed to generate sufficient gains to offset the losses in the value of the Rhythms stock, but also poorly conceived because it relied on the value of its own stock. According to the Powers Report (page 82):

> Swap Sub's ability to make good on the Rhythms put rested
> largely on the value of the Enron stock. If Enron stock performed
> well, Swap Sub could perform on the put even if Rhythms stock
> declined – although the losses would be absorbed by the value of
> the Enron stock. But if Enron stock and Rhythms stock both

declined, Swap Sub would be unable to perform on the put and Enron's hedge on Rhythms would have failed.

In addition, Swap Sub was not sufficiently capitalized and should have been consolidated into Enron's financial statements. During his Congressional testimony, then CEO of Andersen, Joe Berardino, stated, "… in October 2001, we determined that our team's initial judgment that the 3 percent test was met was in error. We promptly told Enron to correct it." In fact, on November 8, 2001, Enron announced that it was restating its financial statements retroactive to 1999 to reflect changes resulting from the consolidation of Swap Sub. The restatement reduced net income by $95 million in 1999 and $8 million in 2000.

LJM2 Co-Investment, L.P. In October 1999, just a few months after the LJM1 and LJM Swap Sub transactions closed, Fastow approached the Finance Committee of Enron's BOD with another proposed partnership – LJM2 Co-Investment, L.P. (See diagram of LJM2 in Figure 5). Although Fastow must have known of the less than stellar performance of the hedge transaction with LJM Swap Sub, he explained to the Finance Committee the benefits Enron received from its transactions with *LJM1*. According to the Finance Committee minutes, Fastow explained that capital syndication was important to Enron's future growth and that the proposed partnership could provide significant syndication opportunities.

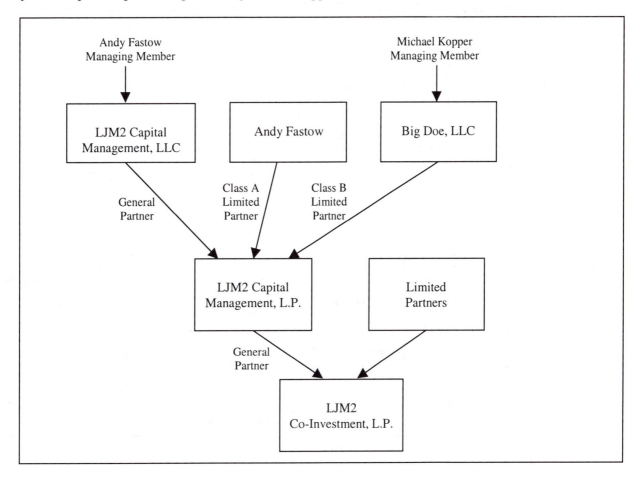

Source: Powers Report, 74.   Figure 5

The proposed partnership, LJM2 Co-Investment, L.P., was similar to LJM1 in that Fastow would serve as its general partner. Once again, concerns were expressed about the potential for conflicts of interest given Fastow's dual roles. Fastow proposed a set of controls to the Finance Committee that would purportedly address the conflict of interest concerns. First, he proposed that all transactions between the company and LJM2 be subject to the approval of Enron's chief accounting officer, Rick Causey, and its Chief Risk Officer, Rick Buy. Second, he proposed that the Audit and Compliance Committee perform an annual review all transactions completed in the *prior* year. Following this discussion the Finance Committee decided to recommend to the company's BOD that Fastow's role in LJM2 be approved. BOD approval occurred shortly thereafter and LJM2 was formed.

The Raptors. Enron and LJM2 engaged in a series of hedging transactions that involved a collection of four SPEs referred to as the "Raptors." (Note: Only Raptor I is discussed below.) As had been the case with the Rhythms hedge, these transactions (three of the four Raptors) failed to represent true transfers of economic risk because they were consummated by entities that had been primarily capitalized with Enron stock. The first of these transactions, referred to as Raptor I, occurred in April 2000 with the creation of an SPE called Talon LLC. Talon's sole purpose was to engage in hedging activities with Enron. A diagram of the Raptor I transaction is shown in Figure 6.

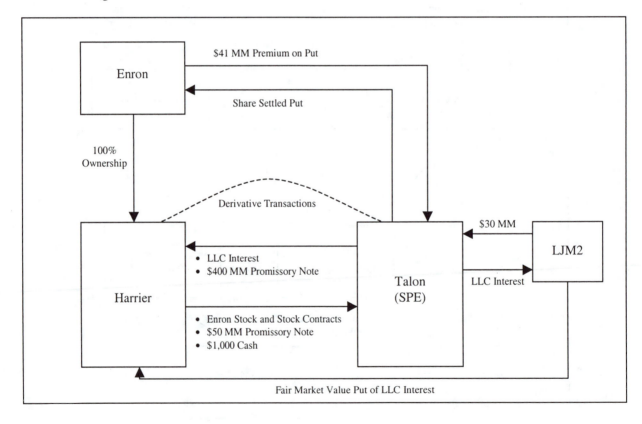

Source: Powers Report, 101.

Figure 6

14

Talon was originally capitalized with approximately $30 million in cash, Enron stock or stock contracts with a fair market value of $537 million, and a $50 million note from Enron. The vast majority of the cash was invested by LJM2 whose only role was to provide the required 3% outside equity so that Enron could avoid consolidating Talon into its financial statements.

According to the Powers Report, "It was understood by those who structured Talon – although it is not reflected in the Talon documents or Board presentations – that Talon would not write any derivatives until LJM2 received an initial return of $41 million or a 30% annualized rate of return, whichever was greater, from income earned by Talon." Even more astonishingly, Enron agreed that if LJM2 had not received this return within six months of the transaction's closing (i.e., April 18, 2000) LJM2 could compel Enron to acquire its interest in Talon. Enron went to great lengths to make certain that LJM2 would receive its return by purchasing a put option on its own stock from Talon for a premium of *$41 million*.

There are two significant issues related to Enron's decision to purchase this put. First, by purchasing the put option from Talon, Enron was betting that its own stock price would decline. Although hindsight suggests that this was not a bad bet, at the time it was far from certain. Second, the put placed Talon in an even more tenuous credit position by requiring it to not only possibly purchase Enron stock in the future, but also compensate the company for the declines in value on its merchant investment portfolio. "The transaction makes little apparent commercial sense, other than to enable Enron to transfer money to LJM2 in exchange for its participation in vehicles that would allow Enron to engage in hedging transactions" (Powers Report, 104).

As the value of its merchant investments began to decline in the fall of 2000, Enron began receiving the hedge protection from Talon that it so badly wanted. However, Talon's ability to absorb the mounting losses was limited by its finite asset base that was composed almost entirely of Enron stock. Therefore, the company took steps to shore up Talon's asset base. First, Enron and Talon entered into a "costless collar" agreement under which Enron would indemnify Talon against losses due to a decline in the value of Enron's stock below $81. The collar also required Talon to pay Enron any gains resulting from stock price increases above $116 per share. The collar only provided temporary relief as the situation worsened. Enron's second attempt occurred in December 2000 when the company created a cross-guarantee agreement that linked together the credit capacities of all of the Raptors (there were four Raptors at this time). This agreement effectively eliminated the credit capacity concerns regarding Talon for the remainder of 2000 and allowed Enron to avoid recording a loss reserve for Talon.

Enron's final attempt at resolving the declining credit capacity issue occurred in March 2001 when it restructured the Raptors. The restructuring was composed of two elements – a cross-collateralization of the four Raptors and an additional contribution of Enron stock contracts. Under the cross-collateralization agreement, Enron agreed to forgo any Raptor termination distributions and, instead, assign those distributions to any remaining Raptor that had a negative credit capacity. However, because there was limited credit capacity in the other Raptors, Enron also agreed to make additional shares of stock available, if necessary. The effect of this latter element was to allow Enron to increase the notes receivable that the Raptors had given to it.

The End of the Raptors. In August 2001, Enron and Andersen realized that the stock sold to Talon in April 2000 had been accounted for incorrectly. In addition, the journal entries that had been made when Enron sold stock contracts to two of the other Raptors were also found to be incorrect. In each instance, Enron had recorded the transactions by increasing notes receivable and stockholders' equity. In September, Enron and Andersen concluded that the notes receivable from these transactions should have been shown as a reduction to stockholders' equity. The combined effect of the journal entries was to overstate stockholders' equity by $1 billion. Enron decided to terminate the Raptors in September resulting in a charge of $710 million ($544 million after tax).

LESSONS LEARNED

Enron's collapse has revealed the less glamorous side of a corporation that was once viewed as one of the most dynamic and successful companies in the world. In the wake of the company's failure, a number of significant issues have surfaced. The following represents a brief overview of some these issues.

Special-purpose Entities
Without question, Enron's failure has given rise to a greater interest in the previously obscure "special-purpose entity" (SPE). Companies often use SPEs to attract investors for specific, limited-term projects. Within the utilities industry, these entities can be used to finance the construction of various projects such as large gas pipelines, hydroelectric facilities, and nuclear power plants. Occasionally investors are willing to invest in such projects, but are not willing to bear the risks associated with the company's other operations. By establishing an SPE in these instances, a company like Enron can provide investors with an investment whose risks and rewards are strictly limited to a particular project.

The accounting for SPEs has been an issue for some time. As early as 1977, FASB addressed the topic when it issued its lease capitalization rules. Later the Emerging Issues Task Force (EITF) published a consensus, EITF 90-15, which became the leading guidance for SPEs. Of central importance to Enron's accounting for these entities is the requirement that an SPE be consolidated unless it is *controlled* by an independent party and at least *3%* of its equity is provided by *outside parties*. Enron treated each of the SPEs discussed above as though they had met this requirement and did not consolidate them into their financial statements. The following is a brief discussion of why the non consolidation was in error.

Consolidation of Chewco. Although there are several aspects of the Chewco partnership that raise questions about whether the partnership should have been consolidated, the requirement that the partnership maintain cash reserve accounts as collateral for the Barclays funding was "fatal to Chewco's compliance with the 3% equity requirement" (Powers Report, 52). Because the initial investment was collateralized by cash accounts, the equity investments of the outside parties were not at risk. Thus, Chewco was not adequately capitalized as an SPE and it should have been consolidated into Enron's financial statements beginning in 1997.

Consolidation of LJM1 and LJM2. In the case of LJM1 and LJM2, there are questions as to whether an independent party controlled them and whether they were adequately capitalized. With respect to the question of control, Fastow was the effective general partner of both LJM1 and LJM2, but each partnership agreement limited his investment authority and, in the case of LJM2, provided for his removal by vote of the limited partners. Thus, it is not absolutely clear whether Enron (through Fastow) controlled the partnerships. The issue of adequate capitalization is clearer. LJM1 appears to have been insufficiently capitalized from the very beginning because its liabilities exceeded its assets by approximately $20 million. LJM2's

16

equity investment was not at risk throughout the Raptor transactions. Fastow made this point in a private communication to LJM2 partners when he said "LJM2's return on these investments was not at risk to the performance of the derivatives in the vehicles, given that LJM2 had already received its return *of* (emphasis added) and on capital" (Powers Report, 130).

Related Party Transactions and Disclosures

In the normal course of business, transactions are presumed to be conducted on terms that are at arm's length. In other words, companies generally attempt to negotiate transactions such that they ensure themselves the most advantageous terms. Although most transactions are conducted in this manner, transactions between related parties cannot be assumed to have occurred at arm's length. Examples of related party transactions include those between a parent company and its subsidiaries; subsidiaries of a common parent; company management; and principal owners (SFAS No. 57, ¶1). Companies must disclose certain details about material related party transactions including the nature of the relationship, a description of the transactions, and other information necessary to understand the transactions' effects on the financial statements. Although Enron disclosed the existence of related party transactions between it and LJM1 and LJM2 – partnerships in which Andy Fastow was the effective general partner, the company failed to provide details of the transactions such that their financial statement effects were understandable (Powers Report, 197).

Another significant aspect of Enron's related party disclosures related to the company's claims that the transactions were consummated on terms equivalent to those which could have been obtained in arm's length transactions. Enron included the following assertions in their 1999 and 2000 annual reports:

> *1999 Annual Report, Note 16* – "Management believes that the terms of the transactions with related parties are representative terms that would be negotiated with unrelated parties."

> *2000 Annual Report, Note 16* – "Management believes that the terms of the transactions with the Related Party were reasonable compared to those which could have been negotiated with unrelated third parties."

"Representations about transactions with related parties, if made, shall not imply that the related party transactions were consummated on terms equivalent to those that prevail in arm's-length transactions unless such representations can be substantiated" (FAS 57, ¶3). In at least one case, there is substantial doubt as to whether such an assertion is reasonable. For instance, Enron hedged its investment in Rhythms NetConnections, Inc., with LJM1 in June 1999, but "the relative illiquidity of Rhythms stock, and the lack of comparable securities in the market" would have made it "virtually impossible (or prohibitively expensive) to hedge Rhythms commercially" (Powers Report, 78).

Auditors "should be aware that the substance of a particular transaction could be significantly different from its form and that financial statements should recognize the substance of particular transactions rather than merely their legal form" (AU §334.02). "Except for routine transactions, it will generally not be possible to determine whether a particular transaction would have taken place if the parties had not been related, or assuming it would have taken place, what the terms and manner of settlement would have been. Accordingly, it is difficult to substantiate representations that a transaction was consummated on terms equivalent to those that prevail in arm's-length transactions. If such a representation is included in the financial statements and the auditor believes that the representation is unsubstantiated by management, he should express a qualified or adverse opinion because of a departure from generally accepted accounting principles, depending on materiality" (AU §334.12). The SIC was unable to determine what steps Enron or Andersen took to make certain that these claims were, in fact, substantiated.

Corporate Governance

Corporate governance principles require the participation of both management and the BOD in a company's affairs. An effective corporate governance structure will result in a well-designed and implemented system of internal controls and the active and meaningful participation of a BOD. Whereas management is responsible for the company's day-to-day operations, the BOD serves in an oversight capacity by providing an independent check on management.

The SIC concluded that Enron's corporate governance system failed for many reasons including weak or nonexistent internal controls, ineffective oversight by various committees of the BOD, and poor communication. The following is a discussion of failures in the corporate governance system related to transactions discussed in "The SPE Transactions" section.

Oversight of Chewco. As originally proposed, Andy Fastow would have managed Chewco; however, Jeff Skilling was concerned about having to disclose Fastow's involvement with the partnership in the company's financial statements and SEC filings. Consequently, Fastow recruited another Enron employee who had extensive experience with complex financial structures, Michael Kopper, to manage Chewco. The SIC found no evidence that the BOD was ever made aware of Kopper's involvement in Chewco even though he participated in a conference call with members of the Executive Committee of the BOD. Moreover, there is no evidence that Kopper obtained, or was directed by Fastow to obtain, the necessary exemption from the company's own Code of Conduct for his involvement in Chewco.

Oversight regarding LJM1 and LJM2. Andy Fastow was the effective manager of the LJM partnerships, a fact that was known, discussed, and approved by the BOD. In the case of LJM1, the BOD understood that it was considering a "specific, already-negotiated transaction" (i.e., Rhythms NetConnections). The BOD approved LJM1 and included in its resolution that either Ken Lay or Jeff Skilling would represent Enron "in the event of a change in the terms of [the Rhythms] transaction from those presented to the Board for its consideration." Notwithstanding the subsequent changes to the Rhythms transaction, there is no evidence that the changes were either known or approved by either Lay or Skilling.
Enron's BOD believed that LJM2 would potentially purchase assets that the company wanted to sell and that Fastow's involvement would speed the process along and reduce transaction costs. A number of controls were put in place to oversee Enron's transactions with LJM2, including review and approval of all transactions between Enron and LJM2 by Rick Causey (Enron's chief accounting officer) and Rick Buy (Enron's chief risk officer) and the annual review of all transactions by the Audit and Compliance Committee. In addition, Fastow represented to the BOD that it or the Office of the Chairman could ask him to resign from the partnerships at any time; all LJM transactions were approved by Skilling; the company's legal department maintained all related documents and maintained an audit trail; and that Skilling reviewed Fastow's economic interest in Enron and LJM.

The SIC found that the "review and approvals" presumably obtained from Causey and Buy were perfunctory. Causey told the SIC that he understood his role to be concerned with making sure that signatures of the relevant business units were obtained. With respect to the annual review by the Audit and Compliance Committee, the SIC found that the transactions were generally the subject of only a limited discussion, often as short in duration as ten minutes. Finally, Skilling's review of Fastow's economic interest also appears to have been perfunctory and ineffective because there was no effort to corroborate the financial information received from Fastow.

The oversight responsibilities exercised by the Audit and Compliance Committee and the Finance Committee were weakened because information was withheld from them in several key areas:

- Rick Causey presented incomplete listings of the transactions with LJM1 and LJM2 in 1999 and 2000 to both committees.
- Andy Fastow presented at the very least erroneous, or at worst, misleading information regarding the investment returns to LJM2 to the Finance Committee.
- Neither committee was informed of the fact that two of the Raptor vehicles were insufficiently capitalized to pay Enron all of the money owed to it (approximately $175 million).
- Neither committee was informed of the growing deficit in the Raptor vehicles or the ultimate restructuring of them.
- On February 5, 2001, Andersen held internal meetings during which it addressed the company's accounting for and oversight of the LJM partnerships. Information obtained by the SIC suggests that Andersen did not discuss these concerns with the Audit and Compliance Committee even in an executive session in which Enron's management was absent.

In summary, there is no evidence that anyone accepted ultimate responsibility for assuring that controls were implemented properly. The most significant problem was the conflict of interest created by having Enron employees function as employees of both Enron and LJM. Fastow was in a position to exert pressure and influence over other Enron employees who negotiated with LJM on Enron's behalf. There were a number of transactions in which employees who reported directly or indirectly to Fastow negotiated with him on behalf of Enron.

Audit Documentation
Andersen was indicted on March 7, 2002, for obstruction of justice, a charge stemming from the alleged destruction of documents related to the Enron audit. Although Andersen has stated that documents were destroyed, the firm has contended that it is not aware of the destruction of any audit documentation. Such a distinction has been lost on many.

SAS No. 96 defines audit documentation as "the principal record of auditing procedures applied, evidence obtained, and conclusions reached by the auditor on the engagement. The quantity, type, and content of audit documentation are matters of the auditor's professional judgment." Examples of audit documentation include "audit programs, analyses, memoranda, letters of confirmation and representation, abstracts or copies of entity documents, and schedules or commentaries prepared or obtained by the auditor." Auditors routinely exclude from audit documentation items such as review notes, drafts of memos and schedules, preliminary analyses, and documents that lose their relevance due to updated information. These items are routinely destroyed because of the confidential nature of the information in them. In the course of a normal audit, destruction of these extraneous documents poses no problems; however, in the face of an impending investigation the documents should have been retained.

David Duncan, former lead partner for Andersen on the Enron audit, pleaded guilty to obstruction of justice on April 10, 2002, in connection with his involvement in the destruction of Enron-related documents. In a prepared statement, Duncan stated, "On October 23, I instructed local people at Arthur Andersen to begin destroying documents, with the knowledge and intent that those documents would be unavailable to the SEC and others. I also personally destroyed such documents and knew they would be unavailable to the SEC. I accept that my conduct violated federal criminal law and am fully responsible."

Self-regulatory Status
Enron's collapse has ended the accounting profession's long history of self-regulation, at least as it relates to the audits of public entities. For the last twenty-five years, the profession looked to the Public Oversight Board (POB) to review the work of members who audited public entities and to impose disciplinary actions whenever necessary; however, the POB terminated its operations effective March 31, 2002. According to press releases issued by the POB, the decision to terminate operations was made after it became clear that the POB would not have a place in the new regulatory structure envisioned by the SEC.

Although the exact structure of the "public accounting board" is still unknown, the SEC has disclosed important information about its plans. On January 17, 2002, SEC Chairman Harvey Pitt stated, "We envision a new body dominated by public members, with two primary components – discipline and quality control." With respect to the disciplinary role, the chairman said that the SEC would decide whether conduct should be pursued as violations of law or ethical and competence standards; the body would perform and publicize results of its investigations; and the body would be dominated by public membership. He also stated that the quality control function would be performed more frequently than every three years by a permanent staff of individuals who are unaffiliated with any accounting firm. Although the final details of the public accounting board may not be known at this time, it is sure to transform the quality control and disciplinary processes into transparent processes whose goal is to rebuild public confidence in the accounting profession.

A FINAL WORD

Enron's collapse has left many of us asking how a company with such apparent success and market prowess could disintegrate so quickly. At the same time, we are also left to wonder how the venerated firm of Arthur Andersen became so terribly entwined in the circumstances surrounding the company's bankruptcy. The implications of Enron's failure have been and will continue to be far-reaching. Accounting standards and financial reporting practices are being scrutinized and many are questioning the effectiveness and the value of auditing practices and procedures. While the future is uncertain, the accounting profession must remain committed to providing information that is both relevant and reliable and it must do so while holding its members to the highest ethical standards.

REFERENCE

Enron Special Investigation Committee. 2002. *Report of the Special Investigation Committee (Powers Report).* Houston, TX: Enron Corporation.

Note: The Powers Report is available at numerous Web sites including many of those in the "Additional Resources" list.

DISCUSSION QUESTIONS

1. Was Enron's collapse due to a failure in the standard setting process? Why or why not?

2. What is the Emerging Issues Task Force (EITF)? Is it the same as the FASB? Does a Consensus of the EITF have the same power of GAAP as an FASB Statement?

3. Should the FASB revise the "3 percent rule" that now governs the consolidation of SPEs? If so, then what level of outside ownership should be required for nonconsolidation?

4. Should a company be required to provide information in its annual report regarding all SPEs in which it is invested? What type of information should be disclosed?

5. How does a company ascertain that related party transactions have been consummated on terms that are comparable to terms that would be obtained from unrelated third parties?

6. Enron asserted that its related party transactions were on terms that were reasonable compared to those which could have been negotiated with unrelated third parties. Should a company be allowed to make such a claim? Why or why not?

7. How can auditors be sure that they have obtained evidence regarding all significant related party transactions?

8. How and why did Enron's corporate governance system fail? What could have been done to prevent the failure?

9. How much reliance should Enron's BOD have placed on Andersen in understanding the company's accounting decisions and policies?

10. When should auditors destroy documents and information that are not a part of audit documentation? How long should an audit firm retain audit documentation? What is a likely basis for such a decision?

11. Do you believe that the current guidance provided by SAS No. 96, *Audit Documentation*, is too broad, too narrow, or just right?

ADDITIONAL RESOURCES

A great deal has been written on Enron's failure, so much so, that one can hardly remember what one has read. The following web sites have a vast amount of information on Enron and related matters.

- Arthur Andersen [www.andersen.com].
- Business Week [http://www.businessweek.com/magazine/toc/02_04/B3767enron.htm].
- C-Span [http://www.c-span.org/enron/index.asp].
- Enron [www.enron.com].
- Forbes [http://www.forbes.com/2002/04/12/fullenroncoverage.html].
- Houston Chronicle [http://www.chron.com/content/chronicle/special/01/enron/index.html].
- "The Enron Crisis: The AICPA, The Profession & The Public Interest" [www.aicpa.org/info/index.htm].
- The U.S. House of Representative's Committee on Energy and Commerce [http://energycommerce.house.gov/107/keywords/Enron.htm].